THE NEW SHETLAND SHEEPDOG